AN HONEST DAY'S CONFESSION

NATHAN BROWN

MEZCALITA
PRESS

MEZCALITA PRESS, LLC
Norman, Oklahoma

Cover Design: Jen Rickard Blair

MEZCALITA PRESS, LLC
Norman, Oklahoma

An
Honest
Day's
Confession

Nathan Brown

MEZCALITA
PRESS

TABLE OF CONTENTS

The Seven Deadly Sins

The Patron Saints

ACKNOWLEDGEMENTS

This is the third book in a trilogy I promised my daughter I'd have out before the end of 2017. Because of current cultural issues, this has been a dark and sad year for her. One that is testing her faith and trust in things. If it sounds like I'm being vague, I am. A father's love is as careful as it is hopeless and bottomless. So, Sierra, here is a book of my confessions for you to see and know that I am not silly or naïve in my love for this world.

Thanks to Carla McElhaney and the *REVEL* newsletter for commissioning and first publishing "By Being Here Today."

Thanks to Jen Rickard Blair for such beautiful, consistent, and prompt design work.

Thanks, always, to my wife Ashley—the best partner and poetry editor you will find.

And, forever, thanks to my parents… who first taught me to confess.

I disobeyed them,
not because I had chosen a better way,
but from a sheer love of play.

~ St. Augustine
Book I – Chapter 10

AN
HONEST
DAY'S
CONFESSION

I
CONFESS

I CONFESS

I want there to be a God.
I don't like the universe,
all that distance and time,
without a him or a her in it.

And I don't care, by the way,
which or what he or she is—
there are several advantages,
and disadvantages, to both.

And if it turns out to be an it,
it will not help the situation
one weird way or another.

I just don't like the "people"
who're in charge right now.
And I crave someone else
to talk to on the evenings
when I don't understand
anything… anymore…
which is most evenings.

MAD INSANITY

I am often filled, ravaged,
with such awe, amazement,
and an all-consuming love
for this pulsating planet,
that I will traipse around
appearing to be depressed
as an odd sort of means to
conceal my embarrassment.

It doesn't make any sense
to me either, so you know.

I have been staring at a pile
of blueberries for ten minutes.
What is it about blueberries?
And it's not just their blueness,
so deep it verges on purpleness.

We have not come into this exquisite world
    To hold ourselves hostage from love.

So says the master poet Hafiz,

some seven hundred years ago.

And because of that, I do believe
he'd agree with me on blueberries.

Now to get even weirder on you,
I'll gaze upon rocks and stones
with the same insane passion.

I spend hours a day on my land
digging… picking… fondling…
cleaning… then stacking them.

And don't start making calls—
my therapist is as skilled as any.

Just remember that our collective
madness may stem from a refusal
to let go to this exquisite insanity.

So Now You Know

I'd rather read *Winnie-the-Pooh*
over and over, and over most
serious works collecting dust
on my shelves—so much of it
fodder for the classical canon.

I quite prefer Shel Silverstein
and Dr. Seuss to 89 percent
of the poets writing today.

I watch old movies, some
of them black and white,
smothered in nostalgia,
when my wife goes out
with friends for the night.

I'll crank up the Bee Gees…
The Cars, Death Cab for Cutie,
Flock of Seagulls, Frankie Goes to
Hollywood, Miley Cyrus—and Mr.
Mister, Pet Shop Boys, Snow Patrol,

and Wang Chung, when no one
else is around… sometimes.

I like to go to nice dinners
and a movie alone. And
I recently ate a can of
Spam® for a late lunch.

Also… I absolutely adore
those little Vienna sausages.

Oh, and don't get me started
on Chick-o-sticks or Funyuns.

Or my lifelong crush on
Olivia Newton-John.

WHEN THE TIME COMES

I think a bit too much
about climate change,
our earth in an oven
set low, until the day
that it's finally toast.

And, I'm not yet in
a stockpiling phase,
but I think about it.

Beans, both canned
and dried… tequila,
a critical part of my
last withdrawal plan.

Those two supplies,
with a water source,
could go a long way.

And yet, if I decide
to upgrade a class,
I might grab some

pickled beets, deviled ham,
and maybe water chestnuts.
You know… a few things
to jazz up a final stir fry.

Also… at some point…
you have to start thinking
about shelf-life. What lasts.

So, maybe some Rice-a-Roni,
mac & cheese, Fritos, Oreos,
Ding Dongs, and Little Debbie
Honey Buns—the prepackaged
foods that never die, or leave
our bodies.
   The reason we
last longer in our graves
now. Good today…
good tomorrow…
maybe forever…
experts aren't sure.

JUST TOO MUCH

The ocean sort of scares me
when I'm out on it, which
isn't often, as I'm from
Oklahoma. But, I have
made it to the Pacific,
the Atlantic, and even
the Mediterranean—
each at different times,
you understand. It's just
that I can only deal with
so much "unknowing"
down below my feet
at any given moment.
Only so many sharks,
squids, or white whales.

Out here, where I'm from,
it's all these fire ants, cactus,
and the diamondback rattlers
that you have to watch out for.
But the first one, you can see
their mounds. The second

is easy to spot, because
it looks fat and funny.
And the third offers
a sizzling heads-up,
when you get too close.
Hearing it once is enough.

The ocean is an unnerving
depth that goes from dark
to darker—until it finally
goes all the way to black.

The kind of darkness
that makes you think
of the infinite galaxies
that're underneath us—
the ones that float always
on the other side from us.
And that is when I begin
to worry about gravity.

POET-YEARS

At 52,
I am old,
in poet-years.

They say we live 7
for every 1 a dog gets.

I'm not sure the separate ratio
for poets, but history says it exists.

John Keats died of tuberculosis
and romance at the age of 25.

Shelley at 29 when his boat,
the *Don Juan*, took on water
in a squall off the west coast
of Italy. Dead of obstinance.

Then Lord Byron, because of
some combination of sepsis,
unsterilized medical tools,
and possibly mosquitoes,

and, let us not forget, sex
with an incalculable slew
of women, and men—

knocked off at only 36.

And so, all considered,
I'm feeling pretty cocky.
Like I'm beating the odds.

Dust to Dust

I take a secret joy
in the misfortunes
of multibillionaires…

though it does no good,
and brings me no fortune.

And it doesn't make it okay
that others feel the same,
as I know they must—

since the news takes
a particular joy itself
in telling us about it.

Oh, they're gonna love
this, they say on sets,
just before going live.

Something in us likes
a levelling… of sorts.

Even earthquakes
and tornados seem
to feel the same way.

Entropy is the word,
I think. That return
to dust and ashes
that makes us want
to look that poor little
plutocrat in the red eyes
and say, *You know, sonny,*

>   *there comes a point…*
>   *for every one of us…*

>   *when the balance*
>   *is finally zero.*

I'll Take Any

I don't want to die…

and it's not as much fear,
as it is love of and for life.

But, there is a little fear.
I can admit to that. So,

if there's a way around,
like Enoch, or Elijah,

I am all in, folks—
whirlwind, a chariot,

I have no preference.

DIG IT

I've always wanted to have
a deep, secret, underground
hideaway only I know about.

A place so hidden, my mom,
with those seventh and eighth
senses, couldn't even find me.

A butane lantern, or oil lamp.
A hundred candles and a cot.
A shelf full of banned books.

A place where the savage sun
of August can't touch me and
the heat index does not apply.

And… where the dirt and I
can talk over the details of
our inevitable marriage.

HISTORY REPEATS

Demons, even Satan,
were, long ago, angels.
For the Bible tells us.

And so it is that evil
incarnate, sometimes
arrives on our doorstep,

having worked up through
the ranks and the legions
of the devotedly godly.

This is why the legs
of the prophets shake
as they sit at city gates,

wishing they'd gone into
law, or medicine, instead,
like their practical fathers
had besought them to do.

This is why prophets are
chosen by God. No one,
who is sane, volunteers
for that deadly position.

So, as the network pundits
and made-for-TV politicians,
but, especially televangelists,
toss us little pieces of manna
made of noise and bluster,

consider what might be
in the silence behind
that off-switch.

God might want
to speak to us again.

LETTER FROM TEXAS
(ON DOWN, ON OVER, AND ON IN)

Some nights, when my wife
is out of town, I go and buy
a jalapeño-cheddar, all-beef
patty from the meat counter
—my wife's a vegetarian—
bring it home and fire up
my grill, then come back
inside to watch ol' John
Wayne and Dean Martin
sweat it out as the sheriff
and a deputy in Rio Bravo
while I prep the meat, and
sip on Hemingway daiquiris
without any shirt or shoes on,
until I take the whole mess out
and slap it over the blood-orange
coals, letting the drip of grease
call up a spit of flames when I
flip it raw-side-down, thinking
how beautiful Angie Dickinson
looked in those black stockings

and lace there in her room
above the saloon while Wayne
tried to keep his cool but couldn't,
giving the bad guys just enough time
to shove Dean Martin's head into
the water trough, then drag him
into the barn to tie him up for
collateral—Texas is still a lot
like that, I think as I dive in
to my hot and juicy burger
on the back patio, where
in July it's still 93 degrees,
sheesh, with the sun almost
gone now behind the live oaks
and cedar, so I strip on down
to nothin' and walk on over,
with the margarita I've made,
to the stock tank my wife bought
and filled up before she left, and
slip on in, neck-deep, to watch
a full moon rise up and over
the opposite stand of trees.

GOLDEN DAYS

If I could go back in time,
I know it would be a very,
very bad idea. However,
I am just dumb enough
to return to the 1970s.

I'd be 5 to 15 years old.
Nixon would be singing
his demise into a hidden
tape-recording system—
and Jimmy Carter would be
on his way to becoming the best
former President of the U.S.

Paul McCartney and Wings
would be holding court over
the crackling metal speakers
on poles at the Westwood
Park Swimming Pool
and Golf Course.
And I'd also be

a hormonally-tortured
preacher's kid trying hard
to figure out a way to hide
what was going on inside
my wet bathing suit while
some girls from my school
slathered every inch of skin
not covered by a tiny bikini
with lotion and coconut oil.

The majority of us would not
yet know the extent to which
a century of spray paint cans,
Freon and combustion engines
had taken our earth's chances
beyond the point of no return—
and summers would be merely hot,
instead of a taste of the Apocalypse.

We would have our Wombles
and roller skates, along with
no Justin Bieber music…

and a planet-wide lack
of Wi-Fi signal. Anywhere.
And, we would not have to
argue over which of the ten
Starbuckses to go to. Whew.

Religion and I would already
be in those very early throes
of our harsh, slow breakup.
What I thought about girls
and what youth ministers
told me to think about
girls, was never going to…
nor will it ever… match up.

The Doobie Brothers would be
helping me build model airplanes
to the tune of "What a Fool Believes."
The movie "Rocky" would make me
obsess to rise above my anonymity.

And in these and the coming years

Roland Lambeth would be teaching me
that comedians come from hard families,
while Dan Hardick would be working out
childhood issues with his last name
up on the world's ruthless stage.

And I'd have monster crushes on Irene
Warwick, Kimm Bedingfield, Lisa Klaver,
Michelle Parrish, Kristi Oldham, Monica
Miles, Lee Mayberry, Kristi Wade, Robin
Tullius, Kelly Fredgren, Katy Hogan,
Kathleen McKenzie, Kristine Kersey,
Lori Yunice, Denise McCarty, Brenda
Turner, Judy Ross, Mary Roche, Kerri
Potts, Amy Neidhart, Melinda Moore,
Connie Eidson, Shelly Dechenne, Duffy
Dougherty, Jamie Bishop, and, my God,
Tane Clark, Jenny Bentz, and Ms. St. John.
And, my apologies to anyone I left out.
But... I either did not have enough
room, or... you were mean to me.

SOMEWHERE BACK THERE

> and what before that life again,
> O God my joy, was I anywhere or anybody?
>
> ~ St. Augustine I. 9.

Was it in some previous life
that I found out St. Augustine
had an inkling of previous lives,
one of many Southern Baptist
heresies of infinite heresies?

I recently had a kind someone
do a reading of my Akashic record,
an act the Baptists would've seen as
tantamount to my eternal damnation.

She told me—among other unnerving
things—that my fists've been clenched
for hundreds if not thousands of years.
And, I barely kept from quipping…
"You're tellin' me, sister…" and,
I barely kept from quipping it,
because few things have ever

sounded so right on about me.
She also said that I have been
playing stringed instruments
for a very long time.   Very.

So now I can't get out of my head
the picture of me wearing a puffy
shirt n' funny-looking pantaloons,
playing a lute in the king's court.
(I'd had me pegged for a jester.
So… this was fairly good news.)

But it also, simply, helps to know
that the extra weight of my heart
comes from so much more than
all the fat and sugar, along with
the pain and anger, of merely
the last ten to fifteen years
that my therapist and I
have been focused on.

MAYBE NOT

Were the benefactress to come along—
    the sugar mama my wife might
        agree to because the deal
           is just too sweet—

I would dissolve my being
into some realm of quietude
where I would read and write
poems all day and play concerts
for myself in the evening hours.
My wife would be welcome too.

In between poems, I might begin
preparations for the evening meal
at around 3:00-ish in the afternoon,
with a cook's drink likely involved.

I would never travel I-35 again.
At least not the parts in Texas.

I would order a professional hit
on my neighbor's lawn equipment,

and I'd pass August and September
at my cabin up in British Columbia
where I would plot my overthrow
of that Billy Collins as America's
best-selling sweetheart of a poet,

during which time I would grow
even more cranky and isolationist
and begin to purchase exclusively
that Don Julio 1942 Añejo that I
will use to commit an unforgivable
sin, by making margaritas with one
of Mexico's finest sipping tequilas.

Which is why I'm starting to think
that the whole benefactress/sugar
mama thing might be a bad idea.

THE PROBLEM IS

I should wait until the last book
I ever write to say this—but
these are my confessions…
so I'll go ahead and confess:

      I do not like poetry.

And by that I do not mean
all… of course. Just most.

Ink-jet printers, Kinko's,
and short-run book services
have created vast vegetable masses
of inert ponderosities—to steal
straight from Lytton Strachey.

There are mountain ranges
of sad if not pathetic attempts.

But, what to do about those few
sordid prophets and seers, the rare

wandering savants mistaken for
idiots, the Zen masters who appear
out of the fog deep in the mountains,

those architects of the soul and heart
whose poems are like drinking
wine all day—slow enough
to keep the buzz, but not
become passed-out drunk.

How small God would be
without the gut-strings
strung across the holes
in their vibrating minds.

FOLLOWING MY DREAM

So, all I did with my life
was to stop in the middle
and start doing what it is

that too many folks wait
till the end of it to realize
they wish they had done.

And, all it took to do this
was a divorce, a thousand
nights without a daughter

that I will never get back,
and the failure to obtain
proper academic employ

upon my graduation as
a Doctor of Philosophy
at my given university.

TENURE TRACK

> that wine of error which is drunk to us
> in them by intoxicated teachers;
>
> ~ St. Augustine I. 26.

As an undergrad...
I floundered my way
through four declared majors
to a bachelor's in linguistics.

As a master's student...
I met poetry, the hot lover
I would go to bed with
for the rest of my life.

As a doctoral candidate...
I learned that learning, like alcohol,
can become a disease—one that causes
the learnéd, when they've had too much
learning, to start waving arms around
and slurring their words, becoming
more impossible to understand.

THE SOURCE

I do not believe in art
as a pleasantry—a mass-
produced poster for offices
of lawyers and dermatologists.

Every poem should have a bee's
stinger still stuck under its skin.

Every smile inside a painting
should have a broken heart
somewhere in a veiled past.

Even a Jimmy Buffet ballad
contains the tweak of sadness
in the backrooms of its verses,
if you've learned how to listen.

All jokes, both good and bad,
were birthed in the bowels
of some ill-fated journey
or unbearable tragedy.

The best comedian I knew,
back in high school days,
was ignored by his father
and berated by his mother.
The guy kept me rolling in fits
and heaves of teary-eyed laughter.

It's why we smile when the bell rings
at the end of *It's a Wonderful Life*—

because Bedford Falls was such
an awful place to live, and be,
without George Bailey in it.

COMPLEX INFERIORITY

Would science agree,
the human female body
is far superior to the male?

As if a creator had considered
the design flaws in a first attempt
and set about fixing the failures?

A man's body's always saying
too much—flexing, puffing,
erecting monuments to itself.

A woman's body is an eternal
Venusian invitation—a divine
art that speaks of and for itself

in some velvety foreign tongue
that far too many men never
bother to learn to speak.

TO SAY, OR NOT TO SAY

> I would say that I had done
> what I had not done.

> ~ St. Augustine II. 7.

From 1998 to 2012, I knew lying
was wrong. But I also came to know
that not telling the truth could help me
stay more a part of my daughter's life.

In 2002, I learned for the first time
that lying could, quite actually,
    save your ever-loving life.

In 2011, I discovered there are
people you don't have to lie to.
That they love you that much.

It's now 2017, and I've found
that the true secret is simply
to keep your mouth shut.

STAND TO POST

It's easy to slay the dragons
of a government too ignorant
to comprehend art's powers.

Just fireless lizards lined up,
like ducks in the stuffy gallery
of the senate's carnival show.

The war is out where artists
fall left and right in the fields
of indifference and distraction.

   Books can be dangerous...
    songs can disturb the soul...
paintings bring chills, or tears.

But those who refuse to read,
listen, and look are the most
deadly force among us.

So, maybe this is it...
the artist's lonely job...

to wage our poems,
set ablaze our melodies,
and brush our very blood
above every doorframe—

to be always at our posts,
locked, loaded, and ready
for each and every soul
that wakes up.

FROM THE ASHES AND WAVES

> …didst of my heart and tongue
> make burning coals, by which
> to set on fire the hopeful mind,

> ~ St. Augustine, VI. 12.

Platitudes and spit-polished sermons
will not save a world with ears
worn out by greeting cards
and beer commercials.

What we need now is
to be licked by the flames
of a dark-tongued honesty that
has gone to hell before us
and returned, without
looking back…

to deliver the news
of what times await us…
the rising waves that lie ahead.

And yet, to do it, somehow,
without dousing our hopes
and dashing our dreams
on those jagged rocks
along the receding
shorelines of
the future.

THUMB-TWIDDLING

Beyond this life's veil,
will our days continue?

But on some other plain—
one with brighter and darker
creatures hiding in the wings?

Will there be nights and moons?
Or just an eternal fluorescence,
like my high school cafeteria
in the middle of summer

when the old janitor
accidentally left all
the lights on during
his two-month nap?

Does anyone else worry
a little, too, about a possible
sort of, nothingness, like
an eternal tranquility

and peace to the point that
you want to claw your eyes
and ears out of your head?
If we still have them that is?

To the point that you begin
to hope that hell will decide
to audit the papers you filed
for your entry into heaven?

But, these are just questions
I ask a bit too often I'm afraid.

Because, I don't know about you...
but I'm gonna want something to do.

If Angels

My wife flew to Miami days ago
to spend time with her brother.

The unspoken agreement was
that she would return and not
leave me here alone with two
feral cats and a dog, one that's
a bit of a pampered princess,
but is terribly sweet about it.

And it's given me the chance
to assess my damage, glimpse
how useless I could become
to this world without her.

Not to put too much pressure
on a good soul. But in these last
few days, I've had more than one
vision of the permanent psychic ball
I might have curled up into there
on the floor of my first house.

Some bad things began to happen—
slowly, and few, at first—way back
around the time I glued together
my last model airplane in the '70s.

The collective psychosis of the things
that humans are capable of doing to
others they once claimed to love,
eventually eroded the relative
sanity I'd grown up with.

And it all culminated in
poor Ashley's misfortune
of meeting me in Memphis,
at the worst possible time.
But… she has stayed.

And though I've made it
a practice to no longer believe
in as much as I used to, she has me
thinking about angels and divine
intervention all over again.

LOSING MY COOL

If the earth loses its cool
altogether, I'm not sure
I'll want to hang around.

It's my favorite season—
the one I used to wait for
at the tail-end of August.

Now, I stand gazing out
the still-warm windows
for most of any October.

Shorts and sleeveless shirts
reveal too much of a man
my age. I don't need I.D.

if I wear them when I go
to the liquor store. Yes,
it takes long pants, and

a coat, for a man to walk
with dignity in this world.
Besides, endless summers

would be like a band of all
and only banjos, or, say…
a symphony of accordions.

I pause and cock my neck
at the mere thought of it.
And think about the way

a good cup of hot coffee
loses much of its meaning
without any nip in the air.

So, I'm considering options.
And for one, I hear that Mars
is pretty cool this time of year.

AGAIN, I SAY

As I said on Page 3…
I want there to be a God.
I want someone with more
pull around this place
to care about it
as much as I do.

I want a creator—
a poet to write, or painter
to paint on a cloud in blood-
red, the oracular message:

> *Hey! I made this! And,*
> *I don't like what you*
> *are doing to it! So,*
> *straighten up… or,*
> *I'm taking the wheel.*

And, I want that cloud
to travel the world, spend
some time in every corner
of every sky, until we've all

looked up from our phones
for long enough to read it.

I want some change.
Change of hearts,
and in air quality.
Change of minds,
and water acidity.
And, even more…
change in leadership.

We need Jesus back…
that ol' longhaired hippie.
Or Gandhi, or John Denver.

We'd even take an illegitimate
son of God—one he'd failed
to mention, because he was
afraid we wouldn't
understand.

A FATHER'S CONFESSION

My dear daughter,

it has always been
how best to help you
on the back-end of things
that never should've happened.

I pick at my cuticles and pop
all of my arthritic fingers
for thought of the fact
that I never made it
in time to stop
the darknesses.

But it was hard,
since I was un-
invited, and so
ill-informed…

to ever pull off
those life-saving,
desperate rescues.

So, of course,
you've now decided
to take those things into
your own hands—which is as
understandable as it is dangerous.

And though I may have failed,
on certain levels, as a father,
I was helped.

              And as long
as you know what I mean
by that, it doesn't matter
that no one else will.

OBEYING THE LAW

I had no idea
the Law of Inertia is
a psychological phenomenon.

But, my derrière in my comfy chair
tends to stay in that comfy chair until
acted upon by some unbalanced force.

And, since my thought-ravaged brain
teems with unbalanced forces, I will
eventually resurrect my rear from
that chair and go outside to dig
up, collect, and stack stones.

Once that motion begins?
Just ask my poor wife…
who has to come outside
with a flashlight to tell me
the sun set 30 minutes ago.

Have I mentioned anything yet
about unbalanced forces?

On rare occasions though,
she'll bring out a margarita
before dark, as a salty bribe
to get me to knock off early,
and I will accept it, graciously,
and sit my derrière in the shade
of one of our beautiful oak trees,
where, as per the Law of Inertia,
she has to come back, again,
in 30 minutes to an hour,
but this time just to laze
next to me with her martini,
because she's both smarter and
more sophisticated than I am.

And that's when I will often
say something brainless like,
*Did you know ol' Isaac Newton
was sitting under an apple tree
when the Law of Inertia
fell on his head?*

THE LAW OF PROXIMITY

There is also a Law of Proximity.
One that I'm likely making up.

It states that those who
are the closest to us
in blood and relation
tend to be those who
are the least impressed
with our professional lives.

Therefore, I'd never assume
that you, my dear daughter,
will ever read these books.

And yet, whether you do
or don't, I should say this:

You are the reason I began
writing a poem every day—
now almost twenty years ago.

You gave me this life and career
I did not know I would have.

You inspired me to share it
with a world that's beginning
to remember that it may need
to not forget about the arts…

the same way it's beginning
to remember that it needs
to not forget about peace,
the other animals… where
the food comes from, and
that sharing it with others
also fills and satisfies us.

And you, I'm so proud
to report, are carrying
that flag into the battle,

the latest battle in The
Never-ending War to

Try and Find a Better Way.

Therefore, you continue
to be an inspiration to me.

So, if the Law of Proximity
dictates your lack of interest
in my endeavors? So be it.

Because I would rather
be close to you Honey,
in blood and relation,
any and every day of
any and every week.

WHAT HOLDS

I may not be the poet
that saves the world…

but… I have a vague idea
of what would happen to it
if the poets ever threw it in.

Even the ones who go unread
are some part of the thin thread
that holds this thing together.

And even those who refuse
to read them understand
what the ocean's bed
does for the ocean.

How, so often, it is
some unseen promise
that keeps it all from falling.

NEVER NOT

Writing a poem a day
is not a job. Nor is it
a discipline, requiring
that I set a loud alarm
or smack a time-clock.

However, not writing
a second or third one,
or maybe four more,
                    that
requires some effort.

It is not that I happen
to notice the dog's butt
smiling at me up ahead
on our morning walks,

the way our feral cat
inches his back-end
forward, without
flinching in front,

or taking his one good
eye off of the cricket,

or the crazy things
people do in cars
and coffee shops,

when they assume
no one is watching
because they never
watch anyone else,

it's that I can't stop
seeing and watching.

I am never not looking.

And I'm never not writing
that next poem in my head.

Coming Ashore

These poems are little notes
tightly rolled up and slipped
through the mouths of dark
green bottles—ones I hurl
into the sea of indifference.

And you, the rare soul who
takes the time to read them,
may wish to disagree. Yet,
you know what I mean.

The weirder truth might be,
I love to think about them,
out there, bobbing in storms
and floating among the sharks
that can't make fins or tails of 'em.

Then, I imagine one washing up
on the shelf of a used bookstore,
waiting for the breakup to happen
that will bring the young woman

holding onto a lukewarm latte
back to the poetry section…
because it's always in back…

where she'll use her left hand
to flick the back cover open,
then a page or two, to land
on this very poem, where

she will come to realize
that someone, long ago,
had written her a poem,

knowing that this day,
this very moment,
was marked by
the stars.

KEEP YOUR EAR DOWN

Sierra,
        of course, I very much
want you to ride out the storm
that your life is… and will be.

Not for a father's selfishness.
But, because I see in you
a bomb of humanity…

one that could go off
any minute, spreading
crystal colors and light,
hope, and its freedom
from the complacency
that's always working
to keep us asleep.

You're the ear of God
pressed hard against earth,
listening to her new gospel,
which, as you are learning,

is the really old one
we had forgotten.

You, and yours,
will make or break
the future of a species
that's made such a mess
of this miraculous place.

No pressure.
And no easy task.

But, in the days to come,
if you ever get bored with life,
I will know it was because
you stopped listening.

VAGABONDO

The persistence of the daydream
intrigues me—like the erratic
hovering of a mad housefly
around my plate of food.

And what I think it's about,
and how my wife would see it,
are two very different things.

And I'm sure my therapist
would see something
altogether else—

if I were, one day,
to start walking along
some undetermined latitude

here above the equator
and simply never
turn around.

WHY I'M NOT A MONK – I.

My mouth,
    according to
    Saint Benedict,
will be my downfall.

I retake a vow of silence
every morning with coffee
and two or three blank pages.

Then, I break it each morning
when my sweet wife wakes up
and passes through the library
to let the sweet dog out back.

        I just can't help it.
        I say something.

And from that point on,
the rest of the day is lost.

WHY I'M NOT A MONK – II.

If you've seen my love,
Lord, when she steps out
of the shower—which my

Baptist upbringing tells me,
by virtue of omnipresence,
you most certainly have—

then you will understand
that the vow of chastity
was out of the question.

WHY I'M NOT A MONK – III.

To give something up is breezy
when you've never had much
of that thing to begin with.

A vow of poverty, therefore,
would not represent a change
for me, let alone renunciation.

All you have to do is add
the letter "v," and then
move the "r" forward,

up in front of the "t,"
and the word "poetry"
becomes... "poverty."

WHY I'M NOT A MONK – IV.

To what... and to whom...
have long been my questions
in the shadows of any vow
I'd take towards obedience.

The Baptists, with their creeds
and declarations—like the Bible
is "100% infallible and inerrant"
with... "thirteen exceptions"—

proved their ignorance and inability
to understand even a quantity
as clear and straightforward
as "One Hundred Percent."

And I was a mere teenager
when I figured that math
all by my own little self,
bless my rebellious heart.

I never stood a pew-warmer
telling me what God told them

to tell me, because I had read
enough of God's biography

to know that, if he wanted
me to know some holy thing,
he was gloriously and notoriously
capable of doing it his almighty self.

I must, however, admit to my recent
vow of obedience to Mother Earth
and her many laws of nature…
because she, it appears…

is going to give me
no choice.

THE
SEVEN
DEADLY
SINS

GLUTTONY – WHATEVER, WHENEVER

It's just that corporate farming
and mass shipping transit
make it so easy now—
the store seems to never
run out of pinkish hotdogs
or chips with a hint of lime.

And so, they are always just
down the road and available
from 6:00 am to midnight
every day, of every week,
even in our small town
of Wimberley, Texas—

which means when I want
my toffee-laced dark chocolate,
all I have to do is burn some coal
to raise the automatic garage door,
and then burn some hard rubber
and petroleum to get there.

ANGER – MY FELLOW MEN

I'm a somewhat jaded soul,
and men are angry creatures.

And that's too much for one poem.
But, I didn't realize it until I was
half way through writing
that opening line.

I was not born jaded.
Nor was I raised to be.
I became jaded, much like
someone becomes an atheist
or a bird watcher… or, say,
a soap-carving enthusiast.

But I'm in recovery now.
Working hard to look for
good in my fellow beings—

and I find that I do my best
when I spend as little time
around them as possible.

Hey… baby steps.

As for the anger of men,
even Augustine admits to it
in his immaculate Confessions
some sixteen hundred years ago.

I did not discover it, any more
than Columbus did America.

But, I am ready to face it now.
Become a better husband. Maybe

set my daughter another example
besides the ones she's seen
from men so far.

ENVY – GREENER GRASSES

These days I mostly want
what others don't have.

I know one man who
has never been sued.
I know a woman who
has never had to worry
about money. She has so
much of it, she doesn't
even need most of it.

Folks who live without
mortgages or debit cards.

And in New York City,
few people ever bother
to get a driver's license.

In Crestone, Colorado,
a shirt and shoes are not
required for service… and
there's nowhere you can't just

walk to, with or without them.
Unless, of course, it's winter.
Then, it's true, you may die.

My friend, Ezra Lipschitz,
doesn't have neighbors, and
he has no lawn, front or back,
because he never waters them.
Ergo… no lawn equipment.

I had other friends once
who lived on the shore
of Hawaii Kai marina
whose air conditioner
never broke—because
they never had it installed.

Anyway, these are among
the many things I wish
I didn't have.

GREED – WHATEVER HAPPENED

I misplaced my greed
at some point—after it
lost its focus on money.

When I found it again,
like car keys by the sink
back in a guest bathroom,

it seemed more concerned
with time and productivity
all of a sudden. It wanted

more days, weeks, months
to do stuff that would never
amount to enough to prosper:

piecing together books of poetry
that few people would ever buy,
let alone take any time to read,

stacking stones into sanctuaries
and altars, ones that mostly only

I offer prayers and sacrifices to,

taking long walks in the woods
and mountains, even city streets,
with no destination whatsoever.

> It's sort of like Obsessive
> Compulsive Disorder for
> the slothful and indolent.

I, the youngest of three sons,
leaving an entire nation of dads
shaking heads in disappointment.

I'm sorry that all I want is to watch
our peppers and tomatoes grow. I'm
sorry I don't mow or water the lawn.

I am sorry that my life's goal, now,
is to come by just enough money
to feed my wife and two cats.

LUST - EVOLVING

Among the capital offenses,
lechery is not the worst—
as long as you're Catholic,
and not a Southern Baptist.

I was the latter, growing up.
And that means I still feel
a twinge of guilt sometimes
upon having carnal thoughts
about my hot n' spicy wife
that I've been married to
for around six years now.

Such is the power and reach
of solid religious instruction.

However, for most of my life
I've also been an avid appraiser
of that often mad fineness found
in the soft shoulders and dangerous
curves, or any of the other pitfalls
that road signs and prophets are

eternally warning us about,
found in the superior form
and structure of the female
gracing the human species.

Roll your eyes… put hand
on hip, if you want… and
deny me the weak defense,
if you must… but… know

that my gaze, albeit male,
is that of an artist—one
of adoration, gratitude,
as well as respect—

and not, necessarily,
that of my rather coarse
Cro-Magnon counterparts.

SLOTH – CAN YOU BLAME

That fuzzy, three-clawed
creature of southern climes
did not deserve to be named
after such an odd capital sin.

The little guy is merely idle
*due to metabolic adaptations for
conserving energy*, according to
the authorities at Wikipedia.

And I myself have no desire
to walk out the front door
during the daylight hours
of August and September
here in the hills of Texas.

And it's nothing to do at all
with a *habitual disinclination to
exertion*, my busy-body friends.

It's to do with the 111° heat index,
and the fact that scorpions and ants

don't even want to crawl out from
under their rocks, or their holes,
or wherever else they can hide.

Today, on the 11th of August,
I am immobilized with my fear
of the no-longer-avoidable truth
that our planet is cranking up
its thermostat out of anger
over our willful ignorance.

And it's getting to the point
I can't even drag myself
out of bed on these
sultry and muggy
oven-baked
mornings.

PRIDE – DON'T TRIP

I am proud to be an Okie.

Look, if you're going to love
a nation, what could be better
than to grow up in the heart?

I even took it one step further
and grew up in the absolute
dead center of the heart
of its heart—Norman,
south of Oklahoma City.

Yes, New England may be
the surgically-enhanced
breasts of our nation,

and L.A. is obviously
our perfectly-sculpted
and well-tanned butt, but

Oklahoma pumps the blood
out to all those extremities.

So, I'm putting you on notice,
all ye stoic pedestrians of Boston
and roller-bladers of Santa Monica:

      Remember why it is
      you still have feeling
      in your fingers and toes.

THE
PATRON
SAINTS

ST. CECILIA

To be a martyr is one thing.
But taking three days to die
from a botched beheading,
seems inexplicably sadistic.
Worse yet, to be appointed
saint of poets and musicians?

Dear God.

But we do need a mother—
one for the road, all the greasy
diners, the bars before the show,
and gigless nights in motel rooms.

Someone to listen to us whine when
the audience is busy texting... and
drinking their two-dollar drafts.

An intercessor—because, even
as good as some of our lyrics are,
we still have a hard time praying.

St. John the Silent

The sun saves us
again, every day, without
making the slightest sound.

And the moon can guide us
back home in the middle
of the night, without
saying a word.

The wide river
speaks in a voice
so soft, we cannot
hear it for our own
footsteps and sighs.

The candle's flame
is quieter than even
the mouse sleeping
at the other end
of the house.

And a breeze
sings so faintly,
we strain to hear
its life-giving lyrics.

To loose the chains
of man-made noise,
we must walk farther
and farther each year.

But, if we're to ever
find and reclaim
our souls…

we'll need
to go there.

ST. FRANCIS OF ASSISI

When you marched off
the road into the woods
to preach to the birds,
that's when people
started to talk.

And yet, God knew
the earth and its creatures
were going to need some help,
once western civilization sank
its teeth into industrialization.

Which makes you my wife's
personal patron saint—since
she prefers animals to humans.

Which is why I've come now
to petition you, in the hopes
that you could convince her
to not give up on me, please.

Because you also happen to be
the intercessor for stowaways.

She doesn't know yet that I
sneaked on board her ship.

Either way, at least do what
you can to save the doves
and the wolves... and
    all their sisters
    and brothers...

from the Republicans.

St. Christopher

Threading my way through
the foothills of the Rockies
with ol' Kevin Welch singing
"Early Summer Rain" as cool
drops of it hit the windshield
here in the monsoon season
of Northern New Mexico,

the thought slips in...

This is it.

I now do for a modest living
what I dreamed all the years
of my youth—I travel...
    singing my songs...
    and reading poems...

and though the dream likely
made provisions for a bit more
of a living than I make from it,

this is still...
pretty much it.

Next year has me touring
both coasts, with a chance
to teach in the Chianti Hills
of Tuscany tucked between.

Were sacrifices made?
Do I have no retirement?
Did I have to carry the weight
of Christ, like St. Christopher,
across some river to get here?

But, with that out of the way,
I venture far and wide enough
these days to think a lot about
the 7-foot, 6-inch, muscled-up
saint, whose likeness I should
soon hang and dangle from
my rearview mirror.

ST. JUDE

No saint would claim me,
so I claimed him for myself.

The sad patron of lost causes,
desperate situations, and even
the Chicago Police Department.

   Most likely because no saint
   would take them on either.

With a club, axe, and an oar,
he's ready for anything, when
I'm out of prayers and options.

Perfect for a man of last resorts.

St. Drogo

Outside the windows of
Milagros Coffee House
in Alamosa, Colorado,
a fairly short and lovely
gray-haired crone stands
out on the corner of State
and Main, holding a sack
of groceries in one hand
and a big "Fire Trump!"
placard, high in the air,
with the wrinkled other.
And, as I sit in the shop,
thinking about the books
Ezra and I have put out,
I invoke the name, Drogo,
our patron saint of coffee,
coffeehouses, and of "those
whom others find repulsive,"
and I wonder... *How long?*
How long will she have to stand
on that corner and hold that sign?

St. Joseph

I too am a father…
dear Joseph. And though
you saw red flags all 'round,
when Mary came up pregnant,
you did a fine job with Jesus.

He turned out to be quite
an upstanding young man.

That's why I come to you
on behalf of my daughter.

If I may be frank… she is
being sacrificed on the altar
of her own frightful beauty.

A lamb that men have been
cutting and gutting as long as
the better gender has existed.

And though I first petitioned
Saint Agnes, she seemed tired

and overwhelmed—there are
just too many young girls
and survivors for her
to keep track of,
let alone save.

So, if you still
have pull up there
in the precinct of heaven,

I'd appreciate, deeply,
anything you can do.

ST. MARY

Your assignments are legion.

Bicyclists, cooks, coopers,
distillers, and fishermen...
goldsmiths, harness makers,
monks, and our mothers—

to cover only a small part
of the list. And so... I do
feel guilty bothering you.

But, I have to tell you...
when my mother is gone,
it'll fall on your shoulders.

I won't know what to do,
where, or when, to turn,
mainly because I won't
know where I am going,
or why I need to be there.

I'll need someone to talk to
who will listen like she did,
which was tirelessly and
with genuine interest.

And if this heads-up
worries or scares you,
maybe you could just go
straight to the source of life
and make some arrangement
for her to be able to stay on,
you know... indefinitely?

ST. AGNES

Despite what I said
in the note to Joseph,
I'm addressing you also.

Because… my daughter is
the starbug that flew into
the corner of the big eye
of my heart's hurricane,
and I've never been able
to fish her out of there.

She is eternally stuck,
and has now caused
a partial blindness
in my peripheral
common sense.

And you…
whether you
wanted it or not…
are her representative
there in the divine court

of intercessory appeals.

You too suffered for beauty,
dragged naked through streets,
because men will likely never
come to terms with their
superior sense of
inferiority.

And so...
by martyrdom,
you have risen above.

You've seen the view
from up there...

and, therefore,
might be able to
tell her what to look for.

St. Genesius

I'm sitting alone at the bar
next door to the Anasazi
(because I'm no longer
welcome there) and in
comes Harrison Ford.

He steps up to the stool
over to my left, and I say,

"O Harrison! My Harrison!
My God... it is Han Solo.
No! Wait! Even better...
Professor Indiana Jones!
You, sir, changed my life!
Yes. You turned me into
the academically-trained
wandering poet-fool of
a treasure-hunter I am!"

And, of course, I said it
as a silent prayer of praise
to good Genesius of Rome,

the patron of actors,
    and of thieves…

because if I had said
all of that out loud?
The guy would've
called for security.

I mean, he was only
after change for a dollar
to plug the parking meter.

ST. ANDREW CORSINI

As you float above the battlefields
our cities have become, riding
your palfrey back and forth
above the demonstrations
and flash-protests where
grown men wear the white
sheets they stole from the bed
they slept in back in high school,
and drunk frat boys march, holding
tiki torches they had to refill after
last night's raging luau-themed
party at the Kappa Alpha house,

>   you understand your task
>   will not be an easy one.

The white sheets represent
cowardice, and a color—
    albeit the lack of any—
that butted in and edged out,
so violently and genocidally,
what we came to call red.

Then, the white forced, violently
and genocidally, what we called
black to leave their homeland
and come to slave over what
we were too lazy and well-
fed to slave over ourselves.

Then, as the white gained
more and more weight,
and so, had to expand
out to the west, to make
room for their bellies, they
had no choice but to remove,
violently and genocidally, what
we called brown back down
to the south of the border.

And now, the brown are
returning in slow waves
to their home, Aztlán,

the black are proving,
defiantly, that they are
proud, and here to stay,

and the red are growing
restless, sick, and tired
of their reservations…

and so, the white're now
throwing sheets over their
balding heads and parading
party favors in circles around
statues of long-dead generals,

because they are terrified
that their time is up…

as they should be.

St. Medardus

We need the water...
we want that rain...

until it never stops.

Hurricane Harvey
has stalled out over
Houston. I-10 now has
twelve lanes of bow to stern
boat traffic.
                        And Noah
has been spotted wading about
along the edges of the bayous
collecting the soggy beams
and driftwood timber
for the great ship
he did not have
the time to build.

St. Mungo

Classes have started back,
and I know from experience
that somewhere out there today
a young boy or girl is roaming
the halls of a middle or high
school in utter confusion
over what it was he or she
did to be consigned to this
nightmarish social wasteland.

Their pain and fear are real,
dear parents and teachers,

and there will be cruelties
committed, ranging from
the subtle to egregious,

pubescent atrocities
that will take decades,
or lifetimes, to overcome.

And, we need to remember
what goes on in those halls
is neither cute, nor funny.

So, he needs you to spot
and keep watch over him,

and she needs an assigned
saint to invoke, one whose
sole mission on this earth
is to protect her from all
the bullies and bitches.

St. Lorenzo

It's been thirty years,
but I remember him.

His name was Casimiro,
a shepherd working alone
in the cold, high meadows
just below Wetterhorn Peak
in the San Juan Mountains.

A heavy white canvas tent.
A 30 ought 6 lever-action,
for the coyotes and other
trouble-makers. And one
razor-eyed, blue-merle
Koolie, who took her
herding very seriously.

We were a wayward band
of backpackers in the jagged
shadows of those magenta cliffs,
afraid to invade his massive space.

He waved us in, though, smiling,
when we got close enough to see.
He hadn't had company in weeks.

And between three out of our nine
who spoke bits and pieces of Spanish,
we were able to figure out that he was
elated to have a human conversation,
even if we weren't all that good at it.

He invited us into the tent with its
makeshift wood-burning stove.
We were cold, and so grateful.

He brewed a big pot of obsidian
coffee, broke a round loaf of bread
he baked from ingredients that were
mule-packed in once to twice a month,
and then killed a fatted foot-wide wheel
of cheddar cheese that he trimmed
a little mold off the edges.

And I am not sure
I have ever had
a better meal.

And…
he had,
absolutely,
nothing else to give.

And…
he had not
seen his family
in three years. A wife
and four kids he sent every
penny the herd owner paid him.

So…
I'm hoping
that you, St. Lorenzo,
will tell his children someday
of the sacrifice he made.

ST. EXPEDITUS

Look, my procrastination might be
just a mild case of thoughtfulness,
good saint of getting-stuff-done,
and getting-it-done… like now.

Taking a test for the sole intent
of getting it behind us, does not
result in learning, my holy friend.

Solutions, solutions. Not every
problem has one, you know.

Maybe it was the Roman,
that centurion in you…

but for some of us,
the peace and quiet
of sitting on a bench
here in the park is more
important than getting our
driver's license renewed. Ok?

St. Sebastian

The system works.
We take hot-headed
teenaged boys, send them
to basic training, where we crush
their identities and grind their psyches
into powder, measure their waist and
boot size, then assign them M-16s
and load them onto C-130s…

and it is off they go to fight
in a country many of them
didn't know existed until
a sergeant threw down
a strategic map.

A country some
will not return from
for a cause we assured them
will guarantee the right and freedom
of every American to purchase, own,
and maintain a riding lawnmower.

It is a strangely, and sadly,
necessary system, though.

One I can't philosophically
argue in a two-page poem.

So, I return to what I said
at the beginning:
                    These
are kids, Saint Sebastian.

You were tied to a tree,
shot with arrows, then
later beaten to death,
which qualified you
as their patron saint.

And so… please…

St. Anthony

So much of what I've lost,
I would never want back…

a few pounds here and there,
the zealous proselytizing
of my youth, and three
women, in particular.

I do not need, again,
my bell-bottom jeans,
or the torture chamber
of 5th through 12th grade
that was cruelly supervised
by 5th through 12th grade girls.

Nor do I wish that "Christian
publisher" I had in Nashville
would turn over the 30 or 40
songs he stole from me by way
of his carefully-worded fine print.

But, I have lost a couple of friends
that I miss, terribly—along with
a lot of cartilage in my knees,
and that 1957 Martin D-28
guitar I was forced to sell
back when I was broke.

That one hurt.

But, more than anything,
I would ask that you help
the corporations and CEOs,
pundits, politicians, presidents,
and prime ministers, as well as all
dictators and other pontificators
of the world. For… so many…

appear to have lost their souls.

ST. VITUS

She never had cause to laugh,
not once, in the first five years
of her life, that one time when,
for most, the world is so funny,

parents doing every dumb thing
they can do 'r drum up to get us
to stop wailing over nothing.

And, as science tells us,
if we skip the giggles
at this crucial stage,
a frown becomes
our future statue.

So, from court jesters
to late-night comedians,
from a good brother or sister,
to that one crazy aunt or uncle,

those masters of the well-timed
witticism have been saving us

from ourselves for eons.

That's why, every time
I watch her face, right after
I take a crack at making it burst
into something else, my heart curls up

and whimpers in a corner of my chest,
dimming the lights in every chamber,
for what it is that I will likely
never see happen.

ST. ADELAIDE

There is nothing wrong
with first marriages working out.
Some people are better at pinning
tails on donkeys—blindfolded—
than others. I hold no grudge.

Shotgun second marriages
are twice as dangerous—
when it comes to our
odds and endings.

That's why my wife
and I took four or so
years to think about it.

We had both missed
that donkey's butt
on the first attempt.

And so, I think it showed
real mental fortitude on her part
to eye me—suspiciously—for what

I remember as an uncomfortable
amount of time, when I finally
asked her to plunge in with me.

She was right to be concerned,
both about second marriages
and the particular person
asking her to try it out.

But, we're six or so years
into it now, and I just wanted
to thank you, my Saint Adelaide,

for helping me to find and score
one of the best second chances
a man like me could hope for.

St. Monica

The world is awash with
the tears and blood-sweats
of disappointed mothers.

Those shed between mine
and Saint Augustine's alone
were enough to first cause
a notable rise in sea levels.

But, wayward sons remain
a key ingredient in the mix
of the mythologies that fuel
the eternal human hope for
learning some kind of lesson.

So, we're necessary vexations.
And, I hope Saint Monica will
one day explain it to my mother.

ST. AUGUSTINE

Half way through Book V
of your sundry Confessions,
by way of all the blood-sweats
and tears of your pious mother,

it appears that a faith in God—
or could we say, Catholicism—
or could we simply trim it back
to religion—became, chiefly,

a means of torturing yourself
in the wake of your conversion.
Your mother got what she wanted,
and you paid for it, in perpetuity.

I will read on, o kindred soul.
But, at least so far? My God.

ST. THOMAS AQUINAS

Please help us learn
that there's only so much
we can learn before we become
useless to society and human need.

I've known academics so academic
they could not remember where
they parked the car, and so,
just decided to never
drive it again—

there's simply no time
to bother with such things
when you are half way through
a 300-page doctoral dissertation on:

"The Lesser-Known Transmogrifications
in the Hegelian Dialectic of the Mating
Habits of Amazon Milk Tree Frogs."

Meanwhile, a truck driver in Tokyo
is breaking his back to load boxes

of the scholar's favorite ink
for his old dot matrix printer.

I was an academic, years back.
And I learned a whole lot about
what doesn't make me happy.

So be with them, St. Thomas.
And help them not to forget
they need to pick up Sally
from school at 2:45—

    and that we could
    really use some help
    cleaning up the place.

St. Benedict Joseph Labre

As I sit in the quiet calm
of my little library, writing
by sunlight this morning,

the hurricane in Florida
is busy making millions
of citizens homeless.

Some for a few days.
Some for much longer.
Some who already were,

but are now so homeless
they have nowhere to go
with all of their nothing.

Two weeks ago, it was
Hurricane Harvey doing
the same to Houstonians.

So much homelessness there,
the news has no time to report
on my friends in the Northwest

who have fully packed their cars
and are evacuating their homes
to be food for the wildfires...

nature's great gluttons that
have consumed hundreds
of thousands of acres—

stopping only to burp,
throw up, and then
start all over again.

Where they will sleep
tonight... many of them
haven't even considered yet.

That's why the real bums
and the vagabonds will
beat them to the punch.

And it's why I have a small
patchwork of friends, spread
out around the United States,

warm homes where I can spend
one night and be welcome, maybe
two, if I cook and make margaritas.

Three, however, and we all start
getting a little uncomfortable.
But still… I am well-versed

in the dark ragamuffin arts.
Florida's more stable souls,
stuck in line for gas, are not.

And, the Federal Emergency
Relief Administration has run
dry of funds and personnel.

So... good St. Benedict—
patron of the wandering
mendicant—I hope

you can see why
I bowed my pen
in your direction.

ST. DYMPHNA

O patroness of the nervous,
where do I begin… as I sit
here, wringing my hands.

Is it true, that you might
understand my blue mind?

O watcher over the anxious,
can you keep me from picking
at my cuticles when in rooms
full of people, or I'm forced
to sit through the absurd
presentations of others?

O caring intercessor of
the emotionally disturbed,
come to me now. Help me
see I might be capable of
loving, and being loved.

O saintess of depression,
what did they do to you…

for you to be given charge
over such a sad dominion?

Dear angel on the hot-line
for neurological disorders…

let's hope I don't come to that.

But… I'm going to keep
your number handy.

Just in case.

St. Luke

The world without artists
would be like the rainbow
without color... curious,
    as a phenomenon...
but missing something.

A leopard without spots,
the tiger minus the stripes,
would just be really big cats.

St. Louis without its arch,
Paris without the Eiffel,
or, New York Harbor
without Lady Liberty,

how would we know
where we were standing?

And, Froot without Loops?
Or, Lucky without Charms?
Or worse... the Cap'n
with no Crunch?

I can't even bring myself
to consider such a life.

So you… Saint Luke,
with your bizarre fetish
for painting Mary, mother
of Jesus, over and over again,

are the perfect patron to watch
over those obsessed oddballs
who fill our walls and halls
with contrast, tint and hue,
melodies and harmonies,

and all kinds of weird
stuff we can't quite
comprehend.

St. Clare of Assisi

With over a thousand channels
to choose from, the plot-meisters
of television now spend their time
on ways to keep our attentions.

And… since our attentions are
permanently divided these days,
they're really just trying—at best—
to keep us from changing the channel,

their channel, where their advertisers
continue to believe that they can
somehow get at least a part
of our divided attentions.

So, as you're aware, St. Clare,
since Pope Pius XII designated
you as the patron saint of television
in 1958, story-lines are going downhill.

Screenwriters have other concerns—
like keeping their jobs, etc.—and,

therefore, we pay, at both ends,
the price of their expert madness.

I don't know—maybe you enjoy
the violence and special effects?
So to you there's not a problem
in need of your care and repair?

Or maybe screenwriters have no
idea they've been given a patron
they can, and need, to pray to?

Either way, we have a crisis
on our hands here.

St. Bernardino of Siena

I worry you've had too much
of the leftover sacramental wine.

You're in charge of advertisers
and advertisement, so I hear—
an odd assignment for someone
who came along before it existed.

Which may explain why it appears
(wine, or no wine) that you have
given up the ghost altogether.

I'd be overwhelmed as well
by a planet quickly becoming
like the poor misguided soul
who just keeps on making
one   bad   tattoo decision
after another, God bless 'er.

I can't answer a phone call
without being reprimanded

for not yet possessing that which,
apparently, I cannot live without.

Billboards now change their minds
and messages every few seconds.

Television is like a protest riot
the police can no longer contain.

And we cover buses in fine print
that warns of serious side effects.

So, if you ever decide to sober up,
I would ask not that you solve
the problem, as much as
obliterate it.

ST. EDWARD THE CONFESSOR

~ for B. F.

My friend is having to let her go.

After twenty some odd years
and five kids, that have felt
like twenty some odd kids
and five centuries, the guy
has done what he could do.

And his heart more than aches,
to the point that the doctors
have told him he'll need
a new one before long.

And I swear, the more
married people I talk to,
or overhear in restaurants,
the more that I sympathize
with your unthinkable plight.

For you to have to
oversee and hear
the bad marriages
and separated spouses
that overcrowd the world,

few saints must desire curbing
human population to the degree
that I can imagine you likely do.

Makes me wanna kiss my wife
every time I walk by her,
and to remind her…

the darkness around us is deep.

MOTHER TERESA

Patron Saint of Doubters

It has to be said. Yes,
this is one of the times
when silence would be
tantamount to a lie...

I've never understood prayer.

The thing religion called me to do
for the answers to my impertinent
questions, for guidance through
those pubescent storms of all
my unrequited infatuations
and the healing of my warts.

You see,
one of the best of my good friends
prayed for nine years to be cured
of the cancer that amputated,
scarred, and tortured him
until he died of attrition.

Joel Osteen prays out loud
in front of his 52,000 fans,
and an audience of millions
on television every Sunday,

then deposits your answers
in his Swiss bank account
every Monday morning.

And so,
it also has to be said
(if the priest hasn't
left the booth yet)

if that's the way
prayer works?
I don't much
care for it.

ANOTHER DOUBT

The writer of Genesis
might have been tipsy
on the holy grape juice
when he said that God
created us in his image.

First... how would he
have known that. And,
second... the evidence
suggests the opposite.
For instance, Baptists
would scold, publicly,
the writer of Genesis,
because God did not
allow drinking alcohol.

And they'd excommunicate
me—usually a more Catholic
kind of thing—for my belief
that Jesus was both a hippie
and a practicing Buddhist.
And that he is, very likely,

the cow standing over
there in that pasture.

The Puritans seemed
certain the Lord was
clinically depressed,
morose, and moody,
with violent tendencies.
And, Catholics still think
the best way to get through
to God is to get his mother
to bug him until he caves in.
Which, as I think about it,
that makes a lot of sense.

And so, I have to say,
if God did create us
in his own image?
I don't much
care for it
either.

BEYOND DOUBT

And so it is, that all those Gods
we created in our various images
gave birth to the denominations.

And, those divine divisions have
caused more righteous sons to kill
their earthly fathers, more mothers

to abandon their sons, and more
fathers to dutifully murder
their own daughters—

more war and violence
than any other construct
in the history of civilization.

And so, I too have to say… if
denominations are religion's way
of doing business? I don't much
care for them at all. Not, at, all.

No Doubt

I doubt that all this doubt
will do a darn thing to help
an aching world that needs
something better from me.

Some hope, in the face of it,
would be braver, more manly,
more responsible as a father.

I heard that you, back when
you were just Mother Teresa,
didn't care much for religion's
pomp and protocol, let alone
being canonized as a saint.

When asked what and how
you prayed, you answered,
Oh, I don't say anything.
I just listen.

And when prodded further
with the ridiculous question,

Well then…
what does he say?

you replied, *Oh…*
he doesn't say anything either.
He just listens.

I doubt that God
has ever gotten more
of a good laugh out of
a moment as absurd as that.

But… see… there I go
doubting again.

Without a Doubt

My doubt meets its dead end,
though, at the immutable point
where I stop to wonder whether
I should be doing this "thing"
I'm doing at this moment—

which may be a strange thing
for a head filled with so much
doubt to hold as a certainty.

But, despite my doubting,
I harbor one hard belief:

that someone, someday,
sitting beneath some tree,

or in the corner of a steamy
coffee shop, or maybe by a fire
of their making, and also maybe
sipping on a Cab Sav (but…

of course… you may
pour any wine you like)
will read this little book
and break a slight smile,

wipe a tear away from
his cheek on the sly
with a thumbnail,

or, shut its covers
and bow her head
down into the deep
encouragement that it
honestly intended to offer.

By Being Here Today

for Carla McElhaney,
written on the equinox
in honor of REVEL

To stay at home—
that's the easiest thing,
I'll go ahead and confess.

Most of us have televisions. So,
most of us know what I mean.

But here we are, despite all
our nut-job days and off-
the-rail lives that, it is true,
we were tempted to let lie
with popcorn on the couch.

Yes, we are here. We have
made it. Reeds tightened.
Journals whipped out.
Ears, and hearts,
unlatched.

So, I want to toss out
something your televisions
don't want you to think about:

If you are feeling hopeless
and helpless in the dark face
of a planet being swallowed
by wildfires and flashfloods,

and a wide world gone mad
with big nuclear grins
and bad haircuts…

by being here today,
you've made a stand.

You answered the call
of the songs and poems
crying out in this desert
of greed and inhumanity.

You have picked up off
the battlefield and raised
again the threadbare flag—

the flag of creation that flies
for the sake of art—art...

the one and lonely nation
left on the bright ember
of a smoldering earth

that has us all
at heart.

AUTHOR BIO

Nathan Brown is an author, songwriter, and award-winning poet currently living in Wimberley, Texas.

He holds a PhD in English and Journalism from the University of Oklahoma and served as Poet Laureate for the State of Oklahoma in 2013 and 2014.

Nathan has published roughly eighteen books. Among them is *Don't Try*, a collection of poems co-written with songwriter and Austin Music Hall-of-Famer, Jon Dee Graham. His *Oklahoma Poems* anthology was a finalist for the Oklahoma Book Award. *Karma Crisis: New and Selected Poems* was a finalist for the Paterson Poetry Prize. His earlier book, *Two Tables Over*, won the 2009 Oklahoma Book Award. He's also recorded several CDs of original music.

For more, go to: **brownlines.com**

ALSO BY NATHAN BROWN

An Honest Day's Ode
An Honest Day's Prayer
I Shouldn't Say… The Mostly Unedited Poems
    of Ezra E. Lipschitz
Arse Poetica: The Mostly Unedited Poems
    of Ezra E. Lipschitz
Apocalypse Soon: The Mostly Unedited Poems
    of Ezra E. Lipschitz
Don't Try
My Salvaged Heart: Story of a Cautious Courtship
To Sing Hallucinated: First Thoughts
    on Last Words
Less Is More, More or Less
Karma Crisis: New and Selected Poems
Letters to the One-Armed Poet
My Sideways Heart
Two Tables Over
Not Exactly Job
Suffer the Little Voices
Ashes Over the Southwest
Hobson's Choice

Anthologies

Oklahoma Poems, and Their Poets
Agave: A Celebration of Tequila

CDs

Driftin' Away
The Why in the Road
Gypsy Moon
The Streets of San Miguel

MEZCALITA
PRESS

An independent publishing company
dedicated to printing and promoting the
poetry, fiction, and non-fiction of musicians
who want to add to the power and reach of
their important voices.